First Edition, 2015, QTR Books

ISBN 13: 978-1503263116
ISBN 10: 1503263118

Book Design by Marilyn Rabetz
www.marilynrabetz.com

BECOMING 70

25 Women From 55 To 95 Discuss Aging

Edited by Gayle Brandow Samuels

QTR **BOOKS**
Peekskill, New York
qtrbooks@gmail.com

First you're young, then you're old, then you're wonderful.

– Stephen Sondheim

There is a certain part of all of us that lives outside of time. Perhaps we become aware of our age only at exceptional moments and most of the time we are ageless.

– Milan Kundera

Living our lives and reaching milestones — whether chronological like a birthday or narrative like becoming a grandparent — makes us all more who we are. An early mentor of mine — Carole Dietrich — described this phenomenon with a smile as the *Moreso Theory of Aging*. The older we become, the more so like ourselves we become. In gathering together the thoughts on growing older offered by herself and twenty-four of her friends and relatives, Gayle Samuels vividly illustrates the wonder and scope of the *Moreso Theory* . Gayle and her comrades are thinking and talking about the questions of meaning and value we are all considering or certainly face at some point in our lives. The very nature of growing older is something of a dialectical paradox — an achievement we all desire: living well to an old age set against the worries of the unknown and the uncertainty of that unknown future. Sharing our experiences, passing on the wisdom of our lives, and finding comfort and strength in our collective contemplation makes us more so like ourselves as well as adding to our ineffable humanity. Reading the views that Gayle collects here made me smile, think, and reflect. I hope you enjoy it as I did and find the worth of the wisdom treasured here for your own life. Be well, stay active, and live long.

– Sarah Kagan

Sarah H. Kagan PhD, RN
The Lucy Walker Honorary Term Professor of Gerontological Nursing
University of Pennsylvania
Philadelphia, PA, December 2014

*A*s my 70th birthday approached, age, specifically my age, captured my attention in a way my previous birthdays never had. There were, I suppose, a host of reasons why it was so that probably included the death of my mother and a close friend six months earlier, but fundamentally it was all about time. Looking back and looking forward I realized that even optimistic reckonings number my future significantly shorter than my past. And while I couldn't lengthen my lifespan, I hoped to shape it. I wanted, as Thoreau says, to live deliberately and, in so doing, to avoid as many of the "I wish I had…" ruminations as I possibly could.

But how to do that, how to avoid the missed opportunities and to fully celebrate the mundane and exceptional joys that scatter themselves across every day of my life was the question that lodged so firmly in my mind that I found myself thinking about it every day and sometimes many times a day. I first thought about writing a blog about aging and the process of letting go and redirecting. But when I realized it appealed to me more because I was eager to learn the responses it evoked than I was to tease out my own reflections I decided to write to the friends whose thoughts appear on the following pages.

They are the women I've turned to time and time again for advice and reality checks, wisdom and hugs and, when necessary, a hit on the head. So I asked: please send me your thoughts about aging and moving on and let me know if you mind having them shared. To facilitate our on-line conversation and to give it a shape and a direction, I posed some questions or comments and my friends responded as always, with interesting insights and this storehouse of wisdom I've read and re-read many times.

This, then, is a collective book: written by twenty-four dear friends and my younger sister. Their ages range from mid-fifties to 90+. They have each taught me something I cherish. They are my wise women and I know how fortunate I am to have each of them in my life. So to each of them I say thank you, thank you, thank you. And to Marilyn Rabetz, who produced this beautiful edition, thank you for what you wrote and for the elegant package-- a beautiful memory house of words – you created; and to Sarah Kagan, who found time in her continent-hopping life as both lead faculty for the Coursera course Old Globe – where I first encountered her - and the Lucy Walker Honorary Term Professor of Geronontological Nursing at the University of Pennsylvania to write the wise Preface to the comments that follow, a sincere and grateful thank you.

- Gayle Brandow Samuels

Nancy

In the same way we think of children as being young, even if they are precocious, I think 90 is old even if we are physically, mentally and socially active. Old is when things slow down . . . movement, speech and thoughts . . . allowing for contemplation, appreciation and gratitude.

Ferris

I have come to conclude that there is no one age that characterizes someone as "old." Old age is a state of being and mind set, not a chronological number . . . I am surrounded by physically and mentally active friends of all ages through 95 . . . Making sure to surround oneself with inter-generational companions to keep . . . engaged and also . . . as your cohort begins to decline . . . and/or die, you are not feeling like the last person standing.

Phyllis

Granted, my cartwheel days are behind me, but I can keep up in the activities that count to me. Cognitive age is another aspect – at 18 I was on a TV quiz show – I couldn't do that today. My recall is frustratingly slow and I am very aware of it. So, in that sense, I am old.

Lois

Old is the face I see in the mirror. I do not let her
define me. We do not spend a lot of time together.

Sevgi

I do not feel old but am painfully aware of my physical and mental limitations which are creeping up. I am now 71 years old. A year and a half ago I was doing what I always do, preparing a multi-course Thanksgiving dinner. By the time the afternoon arrived, I was spent, developed a migraine headache from exhaustion, and had to go to bed. I used to have 20 people for Thanksgiving dinners while working full time so this was the new reality.

Ardis

No age is old. Bodies get old, minds age and spirits can live forever. As bodies fail and minds slip we're reminded that we're not what we were. But is that old? I don't know . . . Our genes, our life experiences and luck strongly determine how we age.

Sevgi

Your friend Ardis eloquently summarized my thoughts, which is that I find so few people who I would call "old." It all depends on physical and mental health. Each organ and tissue ages. As a scientist, here is one example: in bone (my specialty), there are bone cells that eat up bone . . . and [other] cells replace the bone that is eaten. This goes on throughout life in every human being and it is called "remodeling." . . . There is nothing anyone can do about . . . this aging process at the moment, but I am sure scientists will find a way out of it.

Joan

. . . one realizes one is old when all the – or many of the – assumptions about everyday living turn out to be outdated, e.g., when the typewriter you used, or the computer you now use is old hat . . . when the post office no longer exists in your town, when the food stores no longer carry the cereals or cans you are used to buying, when the shoe maker and the watchmaker disappear, and the repairman you have relied on for years goes out of business. On top of that, is the trouble one has learning the new ways of doing things, mastering the Ipad or finding new ways to live without repairing this or that.

Bonnie

I do not acknowledge the age number. I am not yet 70. Perhaps when I am I will feel differently. I hope not.

A new 5 year old patient came into my office recently looking very sullen – definitely not wanting to be here. When I investigated with the mom the possible problem, she said she had told that child that I was her friend Rebecca's grandmother. As the session progressed the child became more responsive. When I sat on the floor with her she exclaimed, "You can't be a grandmother – you sit on the floor!"

Apparently it's our job to change the perception of age. As we have said – it's a number – not a definition of who we are.

Barbara R.

[There is] a false notion that life moves chronologically through stages, e.g., from student life to career and marriage, to motherhood, and, finally, to retirement etc. But what we have seen for a long time, partly thanks to feminism, is that our undertakings need not be bound by notions of what is appropriate or expected at a certain age. Careers change, marriage can happen at any age, entrepreneurs start businesses in retirement, and people get college degrees in their seventies.

Therefore, in thinking about turning seventy, assuming one is not stopped by health issues or finances or responsibilities, it's possible to upend "chronology" and stereotypes of youth, maturity, and old age, and plunge into new experiences. The desire to seize the moment and accomplish what appeared impossible before or just didn't yet happen, can take place at any time. I call these "creative acts left undone," ones that push for our attention. Sort of like a bucket list, but with more complexity and thought, perhaps. Something that speaks to a life's narrative that is still being written.

Barbara I.

. . . within the last couple of months I have been smacked in the face with the reality of aging like never before . . . It seems that quite suddenly I find myself surrounded by friends in my age range who are battling very serious health issues...one friend with pancreatic cancer, another with a malignant brain tumor, another who just lost a 42 year old child to ovarian cancer, and on it goes . . . One can't help but think about one's own mortality every time one comes into contact with circumstances like these...My heart breaks for each and every one of these friends, and I want to be the best friend I can be to each of them . . . At the same time, every conversation leaves me emotionally raw/drained and wishing I could take a "time out." Sadly, setting limits and skipping this disagreeable stuff isn't really possible unless I choose to fade out of their lives just when they need me most . . . Not something I can or want to do . . . How to deal with this aspect of my own aging and the aging of those around me isn't easy.

Caroline

. . . The themes of wisdom and prioritizing and living in the present and to the fullest resonate with me. For the past 4 weeks I have been visiting a friend [who] had a stroke, then another, then another and woke up blind and with cognitive impairments at the age of 67 . . . I leave her each day with tears in my eyes . . . then, like everyone else, I get on with my life, but with an appreciation of how fragile are the things we all take for granted . . .

Carolyn

It was probably around the time I became 70 that I did begin to count the years I might have left and truly understand that I was in the final ¼ (1/5) whatever of my life. Just this year, dealing with [my husband's] leukemia and my exhaustion, I have begun to notice how beautiful the world is (the natural world, I mean). It sounds like a cliché but it's true, nevertheless.

A kind of funny thing, although it may not seem so at first, is that I find myself occasionally planning my memorial service and picking out the hymns I want sung there. Since I won't hear the hymns, probably, I don't know why this is on my mind, but I do love singing certain hymns. It's the Methodist in me, I guess.

Anon

I find that as I think about where I am in my life, and my forward path, I am daily more acutely aware of any opportunity to 'enjoy the good stuff,' whatever that is to me on that particular day.

Carole

Zoe is home from the hospital but not quite okay
. . . Even though I am now talking about my dog, the
issues of end of life, love, letting go do transcend.
When I found Zoe lying on the kitchen floor the day
before, I realized that I was not ready for him to die
. . . I would not allow myself to think about how be-
reft I would be, how empty the house would be and
how the memory of past losses are so intertwined
. . . Zoe is alive and yet, I am sad. I know his time is
really marked.

Doris

I'll offer this provocation. I'm happy to be old in this awful time. I'm happy not to have to see too far into the future: to watch the complete collapse of democratic dreaming – here in the US and abroad; happy not to watch (for too many years into the future) the various lost or newly found cadres of crazed young men (and maybe some young women, too) who crave violence, notice, and something like martyrdom. I'm happy not to have to suffer for too many decades with the newfound technologies and their capacity for overload, pseudo-connections, and no end of distraction.

My children and grandchildren will cope – as best they can. But I don't need to be on the front lines or someplace close in this war for meaning, sanity, work that matters, and intimacy. It's too late for me. And that's just fine.

Gwen

The good thing about time is that there is never enough of it, for anything. As we deal with one problem, joy, relationship, we move on to the next. That, I think is living life so I don't expect it to finish. When death comes, it comes and life will always be unfinished. We do the best we can in a complicated world and are grateful that our basic needs for survival are satisfied so we can dwell on the complications that surround us.

Gayle

Yesterday I watched a Master Class at Curtis Institute of Music. It's an annual event that I have the enormous pleasure of experiencing because it is made possible by a dear friend. As I watched those amazingly talented musicians first playing, then improving their craft under the guidance of this master musician, I thought about nomenclature and how much it seems to shape how we see and understand an experience.

Why I wondered aren't more of us regarded as masters? And, as a corollary, why aren't more of us being asked to share our expertise with younger people? And, as a final thought, I wondered what it might feel like to be considered a master, and whether or not being so designated might, in itself, shape our experience?

Marilyn

As a teacher of a skill based subject – drawing – I have long been regarded, and felt like, a "master." And it is lovely to pass on the knowledge that I have spent decades learning to younger minds. Teaching profoundly reinforces what you know about anything and is extremely rewarding. Our culture should allow non-teachers to have the same experience.

Phyllis

I am thinking not only of how to go forward, but how to assess the life I have led. I would like my grand-children (and, to some extent, their parents) to know about who I was and how we lived before they were part of my world. I am a product of the 20th century, and they of the 21st.

Nancy

. . . one of the things I am embracing with aging . . .
the ability to give things more thought based upon
a bigger pot of experiences to draw from and less
need to give an immediate response . . . that said, the
times in my life that I have worked hard and [gone]
beyond my comfort zone are times I am happy about
. . . I think we applaud true acts of courage within
ourselves and others because we know the cost and
effort involved.

Paula

I had an old friend here a few weeks ago and she said her new view of this stage of her life is "attitude and gratitude." If you think about this it does make good sense. We need to continue to see our lives with the 'right' attitude (positive) and be grateful for what we have had and continue to have.

I see this aging process as our developmental challenge: just as our children had theirs from 1-5, 5-10 and throughout their life cycle. We are now faced with how we work through the challenges of being in our 70s, 80s and so on. There are certainly some good models around, but I think each of us will have to work through our own answers to how we respond to growing old.

Sharon

I'm trying to find new opportunities to grow and learn in ways that will also improve or at least maintain mental and physical health, and not to be too satisfied with the status quo.

Lois

I try to spend more time thinking about my **TO DO** list than about my **CAN'T DO** list.

Joan

. . . an issue about aging that I guess we have to adapt to: it is that ANY decisions one makes, any activities one engages in, have to be understood as "temporary." Time moves faster as we age in a certain sense. When we were between the ages of 1 and 20 (or at least 1 and 12 or thereabouts), we experienced changes almost constantly in our physical and mental selves. And then every change seemed to slow down, especially once we hit 20 or so. We knew who we were, and we "developed" our thinking and our experiences, but we didn't feel entirely changed from year to year.

. . . just as we had large physical and mental changes in the beginning of our lives, the changes in us that are both physical and mental accelerate in our later years.

Which are the "later years?" Clearly we in our generation(s) think those years come later than most of our parents and grandparents thought. (And, I presume that diet and lifestyle really have effected that change for us.) Even so, now in my eighties, I feel

— con't.

Joan con't.

the changes happening much more clearly and more rapidly that I did ten years ago. Hence, my feeling that decisions that I make are always contingent. Sometimes, I find that understanding this contingency paralyses me.

. . . So, the issues are complex. We create our own understanding of what it means to feel useful. Whatever that understanding has entailed, as we get older we still need to feel "useful." If retirement threatens our understanding, we have no purpose in life once retired. UNLESS we have the courage to challenge our conventional understanding, and take on new tasks, appropriate for our situations, which provide new meaning and new usefulness for our life.

Phyllis

[In] 1965 when, as a new college graduate, I applied for a job at Seventeen Magazine, [it's] amazing to recall, but this publication for girls and largely run by women, was pretty . . . anti-feminist . . . I was interviewed by the managing editor (a woman), who offered me a job at a ridiculously low salary with the justification that since I was not a MAN supporting a family, this would be adequate. And the worst part of this story is that I meekly accepted this reasoning. I blush at the memory.

In my defense, after a few months I came to my senses and quit.

Ethel

. . . "70" being the new "50," you are then mistaken about a "future significantly shorter than your past!

Fifty years ago, what did you know? What had you experienced? And yet here you are with much of which to take pride in, built on no life-experience and knowledge, slowly gleaned over years. **WHAT A STOREHOUSE YOU HAVE NOW** to build a future on! How rich is the loam you now have to grow that future in!

Do "live deliberately!", and fearlessly. Open yourself to risk-taking when you find something that stirs your imagination.

I think the most important lesson that I have learned is **THAT EACH DAY IS SPECIAL** . . . not to be wasted on concerns of age or aging. Time enough to deal with that when life fails to present you with a new challenge, a new interest, or a new vista to explore!

Look back only when something from your past delights you in memory, or inspires the creation of yet

another memorable moment to relive, in memory, in your future!

. . . It's my feeling from where I stand, at 92, that just because no one dwells on the fact that time is limited, doesn't mean that we are repressing that knowledge.

We all face examples of our mortality every day as we deal with the losses of dear ones about us . . . oft-times much younger than we.

Anon

I've *always* felt that life is short! When people tell me to not do three things at once or to slow down or to not get tired, even as a young adult I'd burst out with "No! You've gotta pay attention! Life is short and you only get one shot at all this keen stuff!

My parents in particular would say, "Oh, don't work (or play, or whatever) so hard, stop and rest." And my response has always been, "Why? Why not *really* show up? What are you saving yourself for?" Honestly, I have never understood: what are we saving ourselves for?

I do stop and smell the roses – intensely. Heck, I think I even sleep hard.

. . . truly, whether you're 7 or 70, you don't know if you have tomorrow.

Lois

I recently saw a plaque that said: there will be plenty of time to sleep. I think I live each day with that thought in mind and work hard at setting realistic goals for myself.

Bonnie

Perhaps my thought would be that I surround my-self with those who give me pleasure – children and adults from whom I can learn. I appreciate be-ing healthy and can live with aches, knowing they are not life altering. I believe that it is true . . . what doesn't kill you makes you stronger.

. . . I have to admit, I am not looking to step outside my comfort zone. My bravery is focused on doing what I want and challenging my balance issues [from a stroke] on stairs to accomplish the goal.

Phyllis

For me, finding meaningful contribution opportunities has been challenging. When I first retired, I went through training to be a Court Appointed Advocate (CASA), working with families through family court. To say the experience was disappointing is meaningless. It was so bad it challenged all my liberal assumptions – and this from someone who worked for 20 years with disadvantaged and/or disabled adolescents. The social service system, at least where I live, is a disaster. We take children from dreadful home situations and place them in even less desirable situations – either foster homes or institutions. I am sure there are some good ones out there, but not in my experience...speaking of the court system, there were many days when I (volunteer), my supervisor (paid poorly) and three court appointed attorneys sat for hours waiting for [a] case to be called. In one instance we waited four hours before being told that the judge had called in sick that morning!...Later I tried to volunteer at a local college as a mentor to students with Asperger's syndrome. I am licensed and have much experience in this area. No one ever returned my calls or answered my emails. It is discouraging

– con't

Phyllis con't.

At the same time that we are volunteering, we often find our own families in need of our time. This may be part of the generational cycle, in my case at both ends, with an aged parent, a spouse, and children who have needed help at times.

Susannah

Friends are dear – just had one die whom I had meant to visit for some months – damn! She lives on in the Bluebirds here . . . where she helped me monitor the nest boxes in spite of her severely crippled body.

[And] one quick [thought] I submitted to my high school's 55th reunion booklet . . . in response to the question "What is still on your bucket list?" I replied: "Just kickin' that old bucket down the road with surprises tumbling out along the way."

Carole

I remember going to a conference years ago on Death and Dying. The speaker said that only in this country, do people think that dying is optional. There was lots of laughter. Intellectually, we understand about the life cycle and know that we are going to die, but we think it is not going to happen now.

What I find so interesting about where I am in my life is that my quest for learning gets greater and yet my time to do everything gets shorter. My bedside table is growing with reading material . . . at times I just want to read, read, read.

I am also struck with an odd thing. I have played tennis and skied for years and have gotten great pleasure from these activities. Along with this, is the goal of improvement. I have taken occasional lessons, but not in years. Now at this point in my life, I am going to ski clinics [and] a tennis camp and I ask myself [why] . . . have I waited so long to do this? I sometime think there is a disconnect in my brain. Here I am trying to keep getting better, yet I know that my time is finite.

To keep on with this rambling, I have just spent a week in Vermont; a place for me of beauty, peace, quiet and healing. I woke up without anything planned. I had no mail, internet . . . nothing demanding my time, the phone rarely rings and I cherished my freedom and feeling of no responsibility. How can I simplify my life when I am at home?

I seem to struggle with the right balance, time with my family, grandchildren and friends is my first priority, then all of my other interests and achieving a sense of quiet . . . I fell like a kid in a candy store and someone with ADD. I do feel fortunate that I have so many choices and my health. I also know that these gifts are precious and life can change in a split second. So how to manage?

Ethel

What I love about this trip (into the over "70 years") . . . is how each woman seems to have started the trip with oh so different luggage! We are all carrying our diverse living experiences into how we face, approach, plan for, and envision the years ahead of us . . . [this is] an opportunity to see the future through another's glasses!

Phyllis

We are deep into the deconstruction of 42 years on Split Tree Road. It is a daunting task. What I have learned so far:

• Two households cannot occupy the same space at the same time (physics 101)

• Acquiring things is much more fun than de-accessioning them (life 101)

• Women are more ruthless than men in disposing of memorabilia (life 201)

• Some children want all their things: some want nothing (siblings 101)

• Energy is finite at this stage of life! Who knew?

Bonnie

I totally agree with Phyllis's observations. When we moved from a house with a basement and an attic to a house that is ½ the size, my mantra was "when in doubt throw it out." The compromise after exhausting conversations with my husband was to get a storage unit where he can go and visit his stuff.

Delight

. . . the sifting of clothes and coming to grips with the fact that those things from 20-30 years ago will never fit again and will only be appealing as Halloween costumes. But, and this is a big but – neckties fall into the category of art work and life diaries. Paul weeded out his neckties that have been acquired since Law School and have never been weeded before. Two kitchen trash bags **FULL** of ties went out and he kept quite a few. This isn't a quantity I can take to the local thrift shop, so I made the mistake of going through them myself. Beautiful silk ties from Liberty's to Armani which are documented in wedding photos, court appearances, etc. So what to do? I'm the one who couldn't bear to chuck them out. Well, my niece Julie took about half for quilting. Caela's taking another almost half for crafting, the boys want ties that Grandpa wore to Court, son-in-law Eric, who does wear a tie on occasion, got the ones with santas and trout on them, and a few went to the Thrift Shop after all.

Nancy

I love connecting with the earth in all her abundance and kindness . . . no need to worry about mistakes because something else will grow back where a plant has been removed. I love the fragrance of damp earth and today the white lilac tree is in bloom...a treat for my senses and soul . . . I love the joy the garden brings to me and everyone who passes by. Sometimes people stop on their walks or in their cars to talk about how lovely the flowers are. I feel fortunate to be able to work at something that brings happiness. The garden is constantly changing, and at times trees need to be pruned and then there are the weeds. But, I have made a commitment to not use any chemicals so my backyard more closely resembles a meadow than the uniform grass in my neighbors' yards.

I'm writing about nature in response to your invitation to share thoughts about aging...because nature has been one of my kind teachers. I have learned, after many years, to stop trying to swim upstream and trust not only where the currents of my life take me, but that I will have the resources...and/or the humility to accept whatever comes... we are all connected to each other and to the earth.

In the garden the phases of life...happen with ease and grace and the garden continues growing around the knots in trees which only makes them more interesting to look at. Abundance, kindness and generosity are the qualities I am trying to embrace as I weed out fear, criticism and negativity.

Gayle

In April 1987, when my mother was 64, she was diagnosed with breast cancer. Fortunately, the cancer was found very early, had not spread, was easily dealt with, and Mom went on to live 25 more years.

But when she revealed, back then, that she had been on HRT, a possible contributor to her cancer, I was shocked. Mom explained that her GYN had put her on HRT because it would "keep her young." But I, who looked at her through my 44-year-old-eyes, already saw her as, if not old, certainly at the far end of middle-age. I saw her sagging skin, widening waist and slower gait, not the still youthful woman inside her aging body.

Now that I have reached an age when young men offer me their seats on public transportation, I think about what it means to look and feel young. I am always surprised by the seemingly speedy passage of time: is it really 25 years ago that we watched a young Chinese man trying to stop a tank from entering Tianamen Square just by standing in front of it? Really! Twenty-five years.

And as I get up each morning and "put on my face to meet the faces that I meet," I increasingly wonder about the two selves cohabiting my body, the one the world sees and the one that I feel. Our five-year-old grandson told me last weekend that I have "crinkles" next to my eyes. He thinks I should smooth them out. And I think, for today at least, I'm lucky to have the crinkles and all those eyes have seen – but can't it just go on, and on, and on. I'll keep the crinkles, but please serve them with an extra slice of life.

Ardis

I'm hearing more and more recently about how older people want others to think of them. How do others, especially those younger, view us? My friend, Sarah Kagan, who's a PhD nurse with a specialty in geriatric care is writing about the myths of aging that cause us to be marginalized. There's even an idea out there that we should rebrand old age. I applaud all of it. But there's another side too. Our side. Lately I'm noticing what we say about ourselves: "old age isn't for sissies,' 'I can't do that, I'm too old,' 'I'm just not comfortable when I'm the oldest person in the room,' 'all of my body parts are crumbling.' So it seems to me that maybe we're doing our part to keep those myths alive.

But does that mean we should just put on a happy, but wrinkled, face when in public and deny the aging process?

It's true that our bodies and minds aren't what they were once, but there's a fine line between admitting to less drive and stamina and appearing 'disabled.' At dinner with friends last night, we talked about Roz Chast's new book, *Can't We Talk About Something*

More Pleasant? , and that brought on a discussion of being older. Each of us has situations in which we're the oldest one in the room. One person said she avoids being in groups with younger people. Another says she colors her hair to look younger and once she retires, she plans to go gray.

I asked, but got no answer, about whether it's our fear of being judged less able that makes us ill at ease? Or is it a fear of not being able to hold one's own?...If we thought people looked to us as wise and masterful, would we feel ok about being the eldest in the room?

So if we're rebranding old age, I guess we need to include a boost in our collective self-image.

Marilyn

I wonder if it is not just a matter of not wanting to see a person in the mirror who looks older that we feel inside. And women have greater freedom (and personal history) in using makeup and hair color from our early years than men do. As one who chooses to dye my hair, I know that it affects my sense of energy and purpose to see a face in the mirror that comports with my inner sense of myself. For me it is absolutely not about what anyone else thinks. I am not denying my age – I am 69, But I feel 24, and I prefer to look (to myself) 59.

Joan

Ardis' comments remind me that sometimes I look round a room that includes maybe 20 or more older women and discover that only five of us, at most, have allowed our hair to go grey. Others have a light blonde, or almost black head of hair with not one strand of grey or white in it. Their male partners, on the other hand, seem to be either grey headed or have a ring of grey hair encircling their bald crown . . . Why do so many of us women choose to spend our money and our time (which is becoming more and more precious) on changing the color of our hair? Is it that we have been conditioned to believe that we lose our attractiveness to our partners once we admit our age to them? Don't they know how old we are anyway? Or, once we admit our age do WE lost attractiveness to **OURSELVES**? Is it that, having dyed one's hair when younger, some women find it difficult to envision how to face the **TRANSITION** period? Or perhaps we consider that a man's ego will be damaged if he, with grey hair, is seen in public with a woman who appears to be his age or thereabouts?

I always wonder whether some women dye their hair **DESPITE** the fact that their partner admires older women with grey hair?

Carole

My grandmother died at age 85 with grey hair, my mother died at 87 with dyed hair and while I do not know when I will die, my hair is dyed and I am 72. I dye my hair because I like the way I look. I am not concerned about how other people perceive my looks. I will admit that people comment that I look younger, but I think that is . . . related to who I am and what I do. Yes, maintenance of my hair is getting to [feel] time consuming, especially since this is a fairly recent task. However, I am not ready for the alternative . . . grey hair.

Delight

I like what Carole says. None of the older women in my immediate family have dyed their hair . . . A couple wigs though. I dye my hair because I like it better this way. Left to its own devices, my hair would be a fairly mouse-colored grey – not the rich white some of my friends have, nor the dark with dramatic white shocks others have, or the nicely salt and pepper of still others.

I've just returned from my 55th reunion at Smith, and I must say most of my classmates were grey or white and really looked old to me . . . very few with obvious plastic surgery.

I'd say most of my friends don't color their hair, but then their hair is a lovely grey of some shade. So who's to judge: it's all about what makes you feel good.

Doris

These years in which we've been growing older are strange on so many fronts. Elizabeth Kolbert, in a provocative essay entitled "No Time," (The New Yorker, 5/26/14) writes about modern people liberated by technology from so many basic, time-consuming tasks – e.g., food preparation and laundry – with no time to enjoy our leisure. We are either working too many hours or compulsively caught up in self-assigned (and culturally validated) activities that keep us in a state of manic doing. Just as technology seems to have stolen our free time, so it has complicated aging.

For example, more and more, we sport body parts (hips, knees, hearts . . .) that are not our own. Then, too, the world of commerce overwhelms us with ways to fight aging: not just hair dyes and wigs, but whitened teeth, skin creams for every body part . . . I won't go on about the diet clinics, the spas, the exercise routines and yoga retreats, all intended to help us cheat the aging process by (feeling better and) looking younger. In addition, we wear the same tights and tight jackets, trendy scarves and jewelry, big bags, blue jeans and running shoes as our daughters and granddaughters. Prodded by clever advertising and habits of consumerism, we buy into agelessness – even those who don't dye their hair.

Aging is (almost) as real as ever. But the need to deny aging **seems** more powerful than ever.

Marilyn

I don't think everyone who dresses "younger" or does yoga or uses skin creams etc. is denying aging. I agree that if one thinks one is *not* aging, and one does not concern oneself with the psychological aspects of getting older, and the need to accept the next Ericksonian stage of life, then one is fooling oneself. But feeling vigorous and, yes, younger, through exercise and good nutrition, and remaining involved in the world we live in via how we dress and how we engage in the digital world . . . is not *denying* aging. It is living fully.

Sharon

. . . To Marilyn's well phrased response to Elizabeth Kolbert's essay, I can only add that caring for ourselves whether it be through exercise or skin creams is not necessarily a denial of aging, but an effort to prolong life and to promote the quality of that life. In that same vein, though it is not easy to navigate or even understand the new apps and web uses, I try because I want to understand the world in which I live and not to limit myself to the world of my past experience. An example of the significance of [adapting to the] new technology is the experience of my 91-year-old mother who has never used a computer, but now uses an Ipad every day to communicate with her family. This was a life link for her during a bitter winter when she couldn't leave her apartment. Prior to getting the Ipad . . . she felt left out of family news and photo sharing. Now she is in some respects the center of those activities.

Paula

Thank you Marilyn. I was having the same kind of reaction to the recent emails about the "negatives" on doing things that make one feel healthy and good. I, too, do not see exercise, concern about a healthy diet, taking care of your body and, yes, even whitening your teeth as a denial of aging, but instead I view it all as part of smart living and taking care of ourselves. I intend to grow old graciously, but not stopping making myself feel as good as possible along the way.

Bonnie

. . . We are at the end of a trip that made me...more cognizant of my age and my looks (both, by the way, I am not very good at accepting). My husband and I alternate choosing a vacation each year. This year we are at the end of a National Parks trip. We are not hikers. We don't own, nor bought, hiking gear. For the last Parks trip I found the hotels and guides. This year he found a company (Off the Beaten Path) who, with our input, put the trip together. We filled out forms that asked how many miles we could walk and our level of fitness. Apparently they were not read.

The first guide in Zion was 29 and a finalist in American Ninja. That should have given us the first clue. He suggested we hike the river bed of the Narrows. So we shed our sneakers, donned water boots and water pants up to our waists. We walked a mile to the head of the river and walked between and on slippery rocks for about ½ mile of the 15 mile Narrows. It sounds easier than it looks – everyone uses hiking poles. For us this was all a first experience. I walk – I don't hike.

– con't.

Bonnie con't.

The old, beat-up 1993 van had no step, and no hand grip. So each and every time I got in and out I needed to hold on to the front seat and hoist myself up or down. By the end of the second day (same van – different activity and different 29-year-old), I had found muscles that hadn't been awakened in a long time. We needed to ask where there was a restroom for those two days.

The two guides we had in Arches and the Grand Canyon were 60. While they were extremely fit and the hikes challenged our comfort level, the vans had a step, and they asked us about restroom needs.

Perhaps what was most important is that they both said that what we had done – climbing, descending, navigating and negotiating rocks and pushing ourselves to walk longer distances (5-7 miles in these terrains) and challenging our comfort level – we would remember as opposed to the 29 year-olds who take it for granted. My face has weathered, dried and lined in these 3 weeks. I have black and blue marks in unmentionable places, my husband has skinned and bloodied legs, but we did it. Now we are at a resort in Scottsdale because the Sedona fires prevented us from going there. We won't be able to do the hot air balloon ride, but I am going to have a massage and a facial and will dye my hair when I return home.

Phyllis

. . . to the larger issue of aging . . . I have a 94-year-old mother. She is able to walk, talk, see, hear, think. She is financially secure, has a lovely apartment and all 3 of her children live in close proximity. Grandchildren and great grandchildren visit often. She is in two book clubs and has no trouble reading or remembering the books. Two of her neighbors are regular lunch outing companions. Sounds ideal. The reality is that she is angry and depressed and unwilling to take medications. She had major surgery two years ago when she was near death with an aortic aneurysm. Her surgeons had never operated on someone her age and consider the results a triumph. My mother feels otherwise. She regrets having had the surgery, although she faced certain death.

So how do we measure "successful" aging?

Marilyn

. . . how [did] your mother view life before the aneurism? As you describe her she has much to enjoy yet doesn't. Is she in pain?

Phyllis

She is not in much pain, although she does not feel fully well. Her major complaints are about loss of autonomy rather than physical ailments. She is very angry at the loss of control over her life. She probably always had a propensity for depression. What I (and my siblings) see is a difference not in personality traits, but in the intensity and expression of them. Like all lives, hers is complicated. What I meant to convey is [that] the experience of old age . . . is dependent on more than the observable circumstances. I watched my mother's oldest and closest friend live with COPD, tethered to an oxygen line and needing daily chest pounding in the hospital, and yet she was able to find meaning and pleasure in life to the end. I recognize that there is great physical and psychic pain inherent in aging, but how it is experienced and transformed is the real issue.

Marilyn

. . . Yes, in my experience people become more of whoever they always were as [they] approach the end of life. My father became more difficult and my mother-in-law became sweeter.

Paula

Attitude and basic disposition knows no age.

Gayle

I couldn't agree more . . . but the question that has kept psychiatrists, psychologists, spiritual healers and others busy these many years is, is it possible to, if not wholly change, then to ameliorate our basic disposition?

Carole

So many words are being tossed around about what qualities help aging . . . a sense of purpose, feeling fulfilled, being connected, staying engaged, staying physically active. From my perspective there is nothing new that has been discovered. Aging is just being written about more. . . The truth is I do not know how I will be when I reach the stage when there is no recovery from diminishing physical or cognitive abilities . . . I can think about how I would like to be and what I would do, but that is an abstraction. I do not know. I struggle more with the unknown than with the day to day process of aging.

Kathryn

My Mom, Helen, will be 92 in June. She's just darling, cheerful and mostly health except for memory loss which has stolen some of her fine intellect and inexhaustible energy so that she now finds everything electronic impossibly confusing, looks with dismay at most contemporary entertainment, and has trouble keeping up with the current events. But she's happy, wants to live well past 100, nourishes her garden, and enjoys summer evenings sitting on her front porch reading autobiographies and watching lightening bugs.

When I was helping her pack for a trip she took with us to Colorado two weeks ago I noticed a substantial difference between us. Aside from clothes, the toiletries she packed included a toothbrush and toothpaste. That's all. I added in a tube of dry skin lotion, but she said she didn't need it. And then I looked at what I packed. Compared to Helen, my personal toiletries looked excessive.

For teeth – Helen brushes her teeth once or twice a day, never flosses and can't remember the last time she had her teeth cleaned. She has all her teeth and though they're a bit yellower than mine, she's never heard of teeth bleaching. In contrast I have toothpaste, an electric and handheld toothbrush, two kinds of floss and mouth rinse. Every six months I have my teeth cleaned and use white strips periodically.

For hair – Helen said she'd use whatever shampoo we have in Colorado. Her hair is white, naturally wavy and thick. I have low-poo shampoo, shampoo for colored hair, a smoothing conditioner, once-weekly keratin conditioner, mousse for body, Argon oil for shine, hair paste for definition, a hair dryer, straightening iron, styling brush, regular hair brush, wide-toothed comb and a hair pick.

For face – Helen washes her face with whatever soap is available. That's it. She's finished. I have different face cleanser for morning and evening, exfoliating cream, an electric face brush, sunscreen, day moisturizer, evening moisturizer, AHA lotion for wrinkles, lip sun protection, lip moisturizer, eye makeup remover and eye cream. That's before make-up.

For make-up – Helen has never worn make-up. When we were teenagers, my two sisters and I liked to make her up with eyebrow pencil, mascara, foundation and blush but she wasn't really interested. I won't go into detail, but I have a bag full of make-up.

For eyes – Helen wears glasses and didn't even bring a

– con't.

Kathryn con't.

glasses case. I wear contacts so need contact solution, advanced cleaning solution, dry eye drops, two separate contact cases; two pairs of reading glasses and sunglasses for when I wear contacts, glasses and sunglasses for when I don't wear contacts, and glass cleaning cloths.

For body skin care – Helen wouldn't have packed anything, but – at my suggestion - brought a half-used tube of dry skin moisturizer that one of us had given her years ago. For two weeks she never used it.

For nails – Helen carries one old, stainless nail file in her purse. I've never seen her nails painted unless my sisters and I did it when we were dressing her up as teenagers. I travel with several polish colors and topcoat, polish remover, nail files and a buffer.

Helen doesn't do mammograms, pap smears, skin checks, colonoscopies, or cholesterol checks and she's healthy. I do all those things and I'm healthy. The one thing she does worry about? Chin hairs. Who would have guessed? Whenever one of us visits, she pulls out her old pair of tweezers and asks us to pluck them since her eyesight isn't as good anymore.

My mom always looks great. She really does. And so I wonder, "Do I really need all that stuff?"

Doris

We grew up in a time of fewer soaps and shampoos, shorter shelves for oral hygiene, more modest promises from skin creams, and no fantasies about a face that always said "40." We used sun tan oil. We dieted and exercised. But we did not dress like our 14-year-old daughters or dream of eternal youth. Some of us carried more cosmetics than others. But we were, generally, not enthralled to the cosmetics and cosmetic surgery industries. At least not the women I knew. Moreover, reading the ads in the NYTimes didn't suggest an alternative universe that we were missing out on.

Obviously, all that has changed. Most of all, the NYTimes barely figures in the information revolution – and certainly has no weight in the cosmetic revolution. As more products compete for more sales with more promises of youth and beauty everlasting – and of enhancements never imagined a half century ago, it's easy to lose such moorigs as we have: easy to become confused and even saddened by falling behind those who really know how to keep up appearances.

The question of "appearances" is a huge one. It's worth more time and thought than my quick response here to a charming letter, which does open up the question of what's lost (and what's gained) in a commercially unrelenting campaign to keep us buying for beauty.

Barbara R.

Recently, I was invited back to New Jersey University – where I'd taught for many years -- to lunch with the new and first female president, the new director of the Women's Center (which I co-founded in 1973), and the director of funding. NJCU had received a grant from the Newcombe Foundation which will provide financial assistance to eligible female students over 26. This assistance will be overseen by the Women's Center which is approaching its 40th anniversary. I had been asked to brainstorm two plans with the assembled team: a program design for the Newcombe grant, and a gala celebration to honor the forty years of work of the Women's Center.

I spent three hours tossing out ideas, responding to those from others, and having a great time reconnecting with work that had been so important to me in the past. Being involved in this way, with time parameters shaped by me, gave me a chance to be effective and appreciated. These connections, when possible, with work we've loved, in communities in which we have ties, weave threads of continuity into our older years. The role of elder stateswoman can be wonderfully heartwarming.

Anon

In my own life I can see how every year it gets easier, and I am grateful to every woman who went even 10 minutes ahead of me, but still I have my own version of that story to tell. And the story's not over.

Actually the power of women waxes and wanes. I saw (spectacularly beautiful) miniature paintings from the Mughal era [16th-17th C]...depicting the women of the Persian/Indian court going tiger hunting, *sans* men, except for all the servants – elephant mahouts, spear carriers, etc. etc. Yes, in Persia where today the women can't drive and in India where the male bus drivers rape the female passengers.

I wonder if we studied this closely whether we'd see that whenever the power of women wanes, its lowest point is a little bit higher than the last time it waned? That would be nice to see.

Truth is I believe it's not because we're women. I think it's that we're just too capable, and hence scary to people less capable. Isn't that always the way, independent of gender?

Doris

Ever since I retired in 1998 (before turning 62), I've been trying to make both good and pleasurable use of this "time of leisure and freedom." Often I'm too lazy for the task or too cynical to take it on . . . It's easier to be a consumer of good ideas than a producer. It's easier to criticize others than to act.

I'm not ambitious. I respect the unreliability of my self-discipline. But I write constantly — more each year since I've been free than in any prior decade or even two prior decades. Now I look forward to seeing what I have to say and how I will say it. I write to dear friends — smart, serious people — who respond with such generosity that I can't help but feel that I must be concocting a tasty stir-fry or at least a halfway promising one. A couple of times a year, I write to my grown up or almost grown up granddaughters as if they were friends; ditto for my son, step-daughter and my three daughters-in-law. These communications bind us — sometimes more than I could hope for. They're not, I should say, in the line of duty. Rather, they are a response to some urgent feeling or seemingly important notion. There's an element of surprise to these emails (only the beginning is calculated, and sometimes not even that), which makes them special. Surprise is a sleeper virtue. It should not be underestimated.

. . . there are many moments of many days when I'm prepared to say about this time (up to this moment **BUT** not projecting ahead), it's really okay, no kidding.

Ethel

. . . I turned 93 this May and am doing really well (for the most part). On the **PLUS** side...I am still cooking and entertaining, driving, laughing a lot, painting, writing, and living on my own. I am soooooooooooooo very fortunate!

Oh, but there are **TWO** sides! I have lost 3 ½ inches and am now 4 foot 10 and can no longer reach the top shelf in the supermarket, which is, of course, where they keep all the items I need. (I think G-D is having me work my way slowly down into the earth.) I have back problems so I use a cane outside of the house. That extra leg gives me great comfort and a sense of security. I forget where I put things or I lose items by putting STUFF on top of them. And I somehow have misplaced time, because every day seems to be FRIDAY! I lose words occasionally, however if I don't panic they show up a short time later. I, too, am trying to downsize, and sentiment makes it most difficult. I have 68 years (time I have lived in my house) of memories stored in old greeting cards [Ethel designed greeting cards], boxes, albums, boxes, files, boxes, boxes. I have disposed of a great deal, but it's like shoveling sand against the tide.

With all that said, I feel privileged to have lived this long, and G-D willing I hope I will have time enough left to visit all my saved memories. I rejoice in the knowledge that I had enough blessings to fill all those many boxes.

Bonnie Blum

Phyllis Rosen Bocian

Joan N. Burstyn

Lois P. Cohen

Paula Keizler Cramer

Delight W. Dodyk

Doris Friedensohn

Carolyn DeSwarte Gifford

Gwen Gilens

Carole Nagelsmith Greenberg

Nancy Hess

Barbara Irvine

Caroline Wheeler Jacobus

Kathryn Judd Kurtz

Sharon Lee

Ferris Olin

Marilyn Rabetz

Sevgi B. Rodan

Barbara Rubin

Gayle Brandow Samuels

Ardis Shea

Ethel Sinofsky

Susannah

Anonymous (2)

Made in the USA
Middletown, DE
17 March 2015